FOREX TREND FOLLOWING STRATEGIES
By Thomas Carter

Copyright ©2014

All right reserved. No part of this book may be produced or transmitted in any form or by any means, electronic or mechanical, including photocopying, recording, or any information storage and retrieval system, without prior written permission of the author.

ISBN-13: 978-1503365285
ISBN-10: 150336528X

I0405326

DISCLAIMER

Trading forex and other on-exchange and over-the-counter products carries a high level of risk and may not be suitable for all investors. The high degree of leverage associated with such trading can result in losses, as well as gains. the past performance of any trading strategy or methodology is not indicative of future results, which can vary due to market volatility; it should not be interpreted as a forecast of future performance You should carefully consider whether such trading is suitable for you in light of your financial condition, level of experience and appetite for risk and seek advice from independent financial adviser, if you have any doubts.

Table of Contents

INTRODUCTION

Trend following is an investment strategy that tries to take advantage of long-term moves that seem to play out in various markets. The strategy aims to work on the market trend mechanism and take benefit from both sides of the market enjoying the profits from the ups and downs of the financial markets. Traders who use this approach can use current market price calculation, moving averages and channel breakouts to determine the general direction of the market and to generate trade signals. Traders who employ a trend following strategy do not aim to forecast or predict specific price levels; they simply jump on the trend and ride it.

Trend Following Strategy # 1

Time Frame:

30 min

Pairs:

Major Currency Pairs

Indicators:

Parabolic SAR (0.2, 0.02)

EMA 10

EMA 25

EMA 50

Long Term Position:

when the EMA 10 cross the EMA 25 and EMA 50 up from the bottom and Parabolic SAR is on the bottom.

Short Entry Position:

when the EMA 10 cross the EMA 25 and EMA 50 down from the top and Parabolic SAR is on the top.

Exit:

The best time to exit a trade is when the price crosses back up / down through all 3 EMA's on the chart.

Stop Loss

Just below the EMA 50

Trend Following Strategy # 2

Time Frame:

15 min

Pairs:

Major Currency Pairs

Indicators:

EMA 20

MACD (12,26,9)

Rules For A Long Trade:

- Look for currency pair to be trading below the EMA 20 and MACD to be negative.

- Wait for price to cross above the EMA 20, make sure that MACD is either in the process of crossing from negative to positive or have crossed into positive territory no longer than 5 bars ago.

- Go long 10 pips above the EMA 20

- Place Stop Loss 20 pips below EMA 20

- Take Profit is the same as amount risked

Rules For A Short Trade

- Look for currency pair to be trading above the EMA 20 and MACD to be positive.

- Wait for price to cross below the EMA 20, make sure that MACD is either in the process of crossing from positive to negative or have crossed into negative territory no longer than 5 bars ago.

- Go short 10 pips below the EMA 20.

- Place Stop Loss 20 pips above EMA 20
- Take Profit is the same as amount risked

Trend Following Strategy # 3

Time Frame:

Any Time Frame (but not below 5 min)

Pairs:

Major Currency Pair

Indicators:

50 EMA

100 EMA

MACD (12,26,9)

Long Trades:

- Wait for the currency to trade above both the 50 EMA and 100 EMA.

- Once the price has broken above the closest EMA by 10 pips or more, enter long if MACD crosses to positive within the last five bars, otherwise wait for the next MACD signal.

- Initial stop set at five-bar low from entry.

- Exit half of the position at two times risk; move stop to breakeven.

- Exit remaining position when price breaks below 50 EMA by 10 pips.

- Do not take the trade if the price is simply trading between the 50 EMA and 100 EMA.

Short Trades:

- Wait for the currency to trade below both the 50 EMA and 100 EMA.

- Once the price has broken below the closest EMA by 10 pips or more, enter short if MACD crosses negative within the last five bars; otherwise wait for the next MACD signal.

– Initial stop set at five-bar high from entry.

– Exit half of the position at two times risk; move stop to breakeven.

– Exit remaining position when the price breaks back above the 50 EMA by 10 pips.

– Do not take the trade if the price is simply trading between the 50 EMA and 100 EMA.

Trend Following Strategy # 4

Time Frame:

Any (but not below 5 min)

Pairs:

Major Currency Pairs

Indicators:

5 EMA

10 EMA

Stochastic (14,3,3)

RSI (14)

Entry Buy Rules:

Buy when 5 EMA crosses above 10 EMA and Stochastic lines are heading north (up) and Stochastic is not in overbought position (above 80 level) and RSI is above 50.

Entry Sell Rules:

Sell when 5 EMA crosses below 10 EMA and Stochastic lines are heading south (down) and Stochastic is not in oversold position (below 20 level) and RSI is below 50.

Stop Loss:

Recent swing high / low

Exit:

When 5 EMA and 10 EMA cross in the opposite direction or if RSI crosses the 50 mark again.

Trend Following Strategy # 5

Time Frame:

5 min and 15 min

Pairs:

EUR/USD

Indicators:

5 Min Chart Setup:

10 period WMA (Weighted Moving Average)

20 period SMA (Simple Moving Average)

Slow Stochastic (10,6,6 (exponential))

RSI (28)

MACD (24,52,18 (exponential))

15 Min Chart Setup:

5 period WMA (Weighted Moving Average)

10 period SMA (Simple Moving Average)

Slow Stochastic (5,3,3 (exponential))

RSI (14)

MACD (12,26,9 (exponential))

Long Trade Rules:

Buy when the 10 WMA crosses up past the 20 SMA and the stochastic is signaling up (fast line above the slow line), RSI > 50 and MACD Histogram > 0

Short Trade Rules:

Sell when the 10 WMA crosses down pass the 20 SMA and the stochastic is signaling down (fast line below slow line), RSI < 50 and the MACD Histogram < 0

Stop Loss

Recent swing low / high

Take Profit:

Same as the amount of stop loss (1:1)

Trend Following Strategy # 6

Time Frame:

15 min, 30 min, 1 hour

Pairs:

Major currency pairs

Indicators:

SMA 32 (applied to high)

SMA 32 (applied to low)

Parabolic SAR (step 0.02, max 0.2)

SMA 100

SMA 200

Long Entry Position:

- Price must close above the SMA (32) high.
- Price is above the moving average 100 / 200 SMA.
- Closing price of the bar should be higher than the opening price of the bar.
- Price must "penetrate" Parabolic SAR from the bottom up

Short Entry position:

- Price must close below the SMA (32) low.
- Price is below the moving average 100 / 200 SMA.
- Closing price of the bar should be lower than the opening price of the bar.
- Price must "penetrate" Parabolic SAR from the top down.

Stop Loss:

Recent swing low / high

Take Profit:

10 pips – 15 min time frame

13 pips – 30 min time frame

18 pips – 60 min time frame

Trend Following Strategy # 7

Time Frame:

Daily

Pairs:

Major Currency Pairs

Indicators:

EMA 2

EMA 4

Stochastic (5,3,3)

Buy Setup:

Buy when EMA 2 crosses EMA 4 from downside and stochastic (5,3,3) should be below 50 line.

Sell Setup

Sell when EMA 2 crosses EMA 4 from above and stochastic (5,3,3) should be above 50 line.

Stop Loss

Below low of the entry day but it should not be more than 3% from your entry price.

Take Profit

2 x stop loss or 3 x stop loss

Trend Following Strategy # 8

Time Frame:

Daily

Pairs:

EUR/USD

Indicators:

EMA 4

EMA 11

ADX (13) with +DI and -DI

Buy Setup:

- – +DI must be above -DI and ADX (13) > 22

- – Buy when EMA 4 crosses EMA 11 from downside to upside

Sell Setup:

- – -DI must be above +DI and ADX (13) > 22

- – Sell when EMA 4 crosses EMA 11 from upside to downside

Stop Loss

Recent swing low / high

Target Profit

Exit when EMA give a reversal signal.

Trend Following Strategy # 9

Time Frame:

Daily

Pairs:

EUR/USD or GBP/USD

Indicators:

MACD (3,9,16)

ADX (16) with +DI and -DI lines

Buy Setup:

- – MACD should gives buy signal.
- – +DI should be above -DI. If +DI is below -DI and MACD gives buy signal then ignore it at that time and wait for +DI to go above -DI to make a long entry.

Sell Setup:

- – MACD should give sell signal.
- – -DI should be above +DI. If -DI is below +DI and MACD gives sell signal then ignore it at that time and wait for -DI to go above +DI to make a short entry.

Stop Loss:

Recent swing low / high

Take Profit:

2x stop loss (1:2)

Trend Following Strategy # 10

Time Frame:

60 min

Pairs:

Major Currency Pairs

Indicators:

3 SMA

15 SMA

MACD (12,26,9)

ADX (14) with +DI and -DI

Detrend Price Oscillator DPO (12)

Buy Signal:

- The DPO must cross above the zero line.

- The MACD line must be above the signal line.

- The +DI should be above the -DI or just crossing above the -DI.

- The 3 SMA must cross above the 15 SMA up to 3 candles either before or after the upward cross of the DPO.

Sell Signal:

- The DPO must cross below the zero line.

- The MACD line must be below the signal line.

- The +DI should be below the -DI or just be crossing below the -DI.

- The 3 SMA must cross below the 15 SMA up to 3 candles either before or after the upward cross of the DPO.

Stop Loss:

Recent swing low / high

Take Profit:

2x stop loss (1:2) or 3x stop loss (1:3)

Trend Following Strategy # 11

Time Frame:

60 min

Pairs:

Major currency pairs.

Indicators:

ADX (14)

Long Setup:

- Locate a currency pair whose ADX (14) is less than 35. Ideally the ADX should also be trending downward, indicating that the trend is weakening further.

- Wait for the market to break below the previous day's low by at least 15 pips.

- Place entry order to buy 15 pips above the previous day's high.

- After getting filled, place your initial stop no more than 30 pips below your entry.

- Take profit on the position when prices increase by double your risk or 60 pips.

Short Setup:

- Locate currency pair whose ADX (14) is less than 35. Ideally the ADX should also be trending downward, indicating that the trend is weakening further.

- Look for a move above the previous day's high by at least 15 pips.

- Place an entry order to sell 15 pips below the previous day's low.

- Once filled, place the initial stop no more than 30 pips above your entry.

- Take profit on the position when it runs 60 pips in your favor.

Trend Following Strategy # 12

Time Frame:

15 min

Pairs:

Major currency pairs.

Indicators:

SMA 7 (Black)

SMA 21 (Blue)

SMA 84 (Red)

SMA 336 (Yellow)

CCI (5)

Buy Trades:

The following condition need to be met on the 15 min charts to enter a buy trade. If any one of the conditions has not been met, there is simply no trade.

- SMA 7 needs to cross above SMA 21 indicating a change in the trend. It is important to wait until the end of the 15 min candle forming the cross to confirm that a moving average cross has in fact occurred.

- As the same time as the two SMA cross above, the CCI (5) also needs to cross above the 0 line at the start of the same 15 min candle for there to be a valid buy trade.

Note: We can allow ± 1 x candle for the two crosses to occur, example: if the SMA cross on a candle   @ 8.00 hours, the CCI cross of the 0 line must occur either on the same price candle at 8.00 hours or on the 7.45 hours candle or on the 8.15 hours entry. You would enter only when the   two conditions have been met. If the two crosses occur ± 2 candles apart, example: one cross at 7.45

hours and the other cross at 8.15 hours the setup is invalid.

Sell Trades:

The following condition need to be met on the 15 min charts to enter a sell trade. If any one of the conditions has not been met, there is simply no trade.

- SMA 7 needs to cross below SMA 21 indicating a change in the trend. It is important to wait until the end of the 15 min candle forming the cross to confirm that a moving average cross has in fact occurred.

- As the same time as the two SMA cross below, the CCI (5) also needs to cross below the 0 line at the start of the same 15 min candle for there to be a valid buy trade.

Note: We can allow ± 1 x candle for the two crosses to occur, example: if the SMA cross on a candle @ 8.00 hours, the CCI cross of the 0 line must occur either on the same price candle at 8.00 hours or on the 7.45 hours candle or on the 8.15 hours entry. You would enter only when the two conditions have been met. If the two crosses occur ± 2 candles apart, example: one cross at 7.45 hours and the other cross at 8.15 hours the setup is invalid.

Stop Loss:

Recent swing low / high.

Take Profit:

Exit 50% of the trade when 25 – 30 pips in profit (and move the stop loss to break even) and exit the remaining 50% when a candle closes below the SMA 7.

Trend Following Strategy # 13

Time Frame:

Daily

Pairs:

Major Currency Pairs

Indicators:

SMA 150

Stochastic (8,3,3)

RSI (3)

Long Entry Position:

when the price is above SMA 150 wait for the RSI to plunge below 20. Then look at Stochastic – once the Stochastic line crossover occur and it is (must be) below 30 – enter long with a new price.

Short Entry Position:

when the price is below SMA 150 wait for the RSI to go above 80. Then if shortly after you see a Stochastic lines crossover above 70 – enter short with a new price.

Stop Loss:

Recent swing low / high.

Take Profit:

3 x stop loss (1:3)

Trend Following Strategy # 14

Time Frame:

4H and Daily

Pairs:

EUR/USD and GBP/USD

Indicators:

EMA 5

EMA 15

EMA 50

EMA 100

MACD (12,26,9)

Enter Long Position:

- EMA 5 crosses up EMA 15

- Price is above EMA 50 and EMA 100

- MACD > 0

Enter Short Position:

- EMA 5 crosses down EMA 15

- Price is below EMA 50 and EMA 100

- MACD < 0

Note: do not trade when the price is between EMA 50 and EMA 100

Stop Loss:

Place stop loss on the EMA 50

Take Profit:

Exit position when EMA 5 and EMA 15 crosses in opposite direction or

<u>4H Time Frame:</u>

EUR/USD = 60 pips

GBP/USD = 70 pips

<u>Daily Time Frame:</u>

EUR/USD = 200 pips

GBP/USD = 250 pips

Trend Following Strategy # 15

Time Frame:

60 min and 15 min

Pairs:

EUR/USD

Indicators:

EMA 5

EMA 100

Long Position:

EMA 5 > EMA 100 on the 60 min chart.

Enter long when EMA 5 crosses EMA 100 upwards on the 15 min chart.

Short Position:

EMA 5 < EMA 100 on the 60 min chart.

Enter short when EMA 5 crosses EMA 100 downward on the 15 min chart.

Stop Loss:

Recent swing low / high

Target Profit:

30 pips

Trend Following Strategy # 16

Time Frame:

15-min, 1H, 4H, Daily

Pairs:

EUR/USD, GBP/USD, USD/CHF, EUR/JPY, USD/JPY

Indicators:

EMA 7 (black color)

EMA 21 (blue color)

Rules for Buy Signals:

- First we need to confirm that we are in a strong uptrend. The criteria for determining that price is in a strong uptrend are as follows:

    1. The EMA 7 is above EMA 21.

    2. The EMA 21 line is either rising or flat (that means the slope of EMA 21 line is up).

    3. Price must be trading above both EMA 7 and EMA 21.

- Once we are sure that we have an uptrend, we wait for price to pull-back (retrace). Price declines from above the EMA lines to enter the area between two EMA lines. Then one or more bars touch EMA 21 (or decline slightly below EMA 21).

- Once one or more bars touch EMA 21 (or decline slightly below EMA 21), we place a Buy order 1 pip above the High of the last bar. When price break above the High of the last bar by 1 pip we enter Buy trade.

Rules for Sell Signals:

- First we need to confirm that we are in a strong downtrend.

28

The criteria for determining that price is in a strong downtrend are as follows:

1. The EMA 7 is below EMA 21

2. The EMA 21 is either falling or flat (that means the slope of EMA 21 is down).

3. Price must be trading below both EMA 7 and EMA 21.

- Once we are sure that we have a downtrend, we wait for price to pull-back (retrace). Price rises from below the two EMA lines to enter the area between two EMA lines. Then one or more bars touch EMA 21 (or rise slightly above EMA 21).

- Once one or more bars touch EMA 21 (or rise slightly above EMA 21), we place a Sell order 1 pip below the Low of the preceding bar. When price breaks below the Low of the preceding bar by 1 pip, we enter a Sell trade.

Stop Loss:

Recent swing low / high

Take Profit:

Profit = 2 x Stop Loss

Trend Following Strategy # 17

Time Frame:

15-min, 1H, 4H, Daily

Pairs:

EUR/USD, GBP/USD, USD/CHF, EUR/JPY, USD/JPY

Indicators:

EMA 18

ADX (12)

Rules for Buy Signals:

- Price is in uptrend and ADX (12) value is greater than 25.

- Price declines in a pull-back (retracement) and touches EMA 18. But at the first bar when price touches EMA 18, ADX (12) value is still greater than 25. (This ADX requirement is only applied for the first bar when price begins to touches EMA 18 – for subsequent bars, ADX value could be lower than 25).

- Once price touches (or penetrate slightly) EMA 18, we place a buy order 1 pip above the High of the preceding bar by 1 pip, we enter a Buy trade.

Rules for Sell Signals:

- Price is in downtrend and ADX (12) value is greater than 25.

- Price rises in a rally (retracement) and touches EMA 18. But at the first bar when price touches EMA 18, ADX (12) value is still greater than 25. (This ADX requirement is only applied for the first bar when price begins to touches EMA 18 – for subsequent bars, ADX value could be lower than 25).

- Once price touches (or penetrate slightly) EMA 18, we place a sell order 1 pip below the Low of the preceding bar. When price breaks below the Low of the preceding bar by 1 pip, we enter a Sell trade.

Stop Loss:

Recent swing low / high.

Take Profit:

We place our target profit at the last swing high / low.

Trend Following Strategy # 18

Time Frame:

4H and Daily

Pairs:

GBP/USD and GBP/JPY

Indicators:

EMA 6

EMA 13

MACD (12,26,9)

Parabolic SAR (0.02, 0.2)

Long Entry:

- EMA 6 crosses above the EMA 13

- MACD > 0

- The Parabolic SAR dot is under the candle indicating an uptrend.

Short Entry:

- EMA 6 crosses below the EMA 13

- MACD < 0

- The Parabolic SAR dot is above the candle indicating a downtrend.

Stop Loss:

<u>4H Chart:</u>

GBP/USD = 70 pips

GBP/JPY = 90 pips

<u>Daily:</u>

GBP/USD = 100 pips

GBP/JPY = 150 pips

Take Profit:

4H Chart:

GBP/USD = 60 pips

GBP/JPY = 80 pips

Daily Chart:

GBP/USD = 280 pips

GBP/JPY = 320 pips

Trend Following Strategy # 19

Time Frame:

15 min

Pairs:

EUR/USD

Indicators:

Schaff Trend Cycle

EMA 100

Stochastic (21,9,9)

Rules for Long Trade:

- The EMA 100 is sloping up.

- Wait for the Schaff Trend Cycle to reach oversold territory on the chart (-10+10), go long when the Schaff Trend Cycle turns back above +10, and stochastic crosses line up.

- Place stop loss below the most recent swing low.

- Take Profit: close the trade if the Schaff Trend Cycle indicators goes below 90.

Rules for Short Trade:

- The EMA 100 is sloping down.

- Wait for the Schaff Trend Cycle to reach overbought territory on the chart (90-110), go short when the Schaff Trend Cycle turns back below 90 and stochastic crosses line down.

- Place stop loss above the most recent swing high.

- Take Profit: close the trade if the Schaff Trend Cycle indicator moves down to -10 and then rise back above +10.

Trend Following Strategy # 20

Time Frame:

4H and Daily

Pairs:

EUR/USD, GBP/USD, USD/CHF

Indicators:

4 EMA

10 EMA

ADX (28) with +DI and -DI

MACD (5,10,4)

Long Entry Position:

+DI must be above -DI

When 4 EMA crosses 10 EMA from downside to upside and MACD > 0

Short Entry Position:

-DI must be above +DI

When 4 EMA crosses 10 EMA from upside to downside and MACD < 0

Stop Loss:

Recent swing low / high

Take Profit:

<u>4H Time Frame:</u>

EUR/USD = 60 pips

GBP/USD = 70 pips

USD/CHF = 40 pips

Daily Time Frame:

EUR/USD = 200 pips

GBP/USD = 250 pips

USD/CHF = 150 pips

FINAL WORDS

Thank you for downloading this book. I hope this book was able to help you to jump start your forex trading adventure. If you enjoyed this book, please take the time to share your thoughts and post a review on amazon. It's be greatly appreciated !

I wish you all the best with trading,

Thomas Carter

thomascarterbook.blogspot.com